THE WORLD OF DINOSAURS

BRACHIOSAURUS

BY REBECCA SABELKO

EPIC

BELLWETHER MEDIA • MINNEAPOLIS, MN

EPIC

EPIC BOOKS are no ordinary books. They burst with intense action, high-speed heroics, and shadows of the unknown. Are you ready for an Epic adventure?

This edition first published in 2022 by Bellwether Media, Inc.

No part of this publication may be reproduced in whole or in part without written permission of the publisher. For information regarding permission, write to Bellwether Media, Inc., Attention: Permissions Department, 6012 Blue Circle Drive, Minnetonka, MN 55343.

Library of Congress Cataloging-in-Publication Data

Names: Sabelko, Rebecca, author.
Title: Brachiosaurus / by Rebecca Sabelko.
Description: Minneapolis, MN : Bellwether Media, 2022. | Series: The world of dinosaurs | Includes bibliographical references and index. | Audience: Ages 7-12 | Audience: Grades 2-3 | Summary: "Engaging images accompany information about the brachiosaurus. The combination of high-interest subject matter and light text is intended for students in grades 2 through 7"-- Provided by publisher.
Identifiers: LCCN 2021022415 (print) | LCCN 2021022416 (ebook) | ISBN 9781644875438 (library binding) | ISBN 9781648344992 (paperback) | ISBN 9781648344510 (ebook)
Subjects: LCSH: Brachiosaurus--Juvenile literature.
Classification: LCC QE862.S3 S23226 2022 (print) | LCC QE862.S3 (ebook) | DDC 567.913--dc23
LC record available at https://lccn.loc.gov/2021022415
LC ebook record available at https://lccn.loc.gov/2021022416

Text copyright © 2022 by Bellwether Media, Inc. EPIC and associated logos are trademarks and/or registered trademarks of Bellwether Media, Inc.

Editor: Betsy Rathburn   Designer: Jeffrey Kollock

Printed in the United States of America, North Mankato, MN.

TABLE OF CONTENTS

THE WORLD OF THE BRACHIOSAURUS	4
WHAT WAS THE BRACHIOSAURUS?	6
DIET AND DEFENSES	12
FOSSILS AND EXTINCTION	16
GET TO KNOW THE BRACHIOSAURUS	20
GLOSSARY	22
TO LEARN MORE	23
INDEX	24

THE WORLD OF THE BRACHIOSAURUS

PRONUNCIATION

BRAK-ee-oh-SORE-us

The brachiosaurus was a huge dinosaur. Its long neck helped it hold its head up high!

⚠️ MAP OF THE WORLD

Late Jurassic period

It lived around 152 million years ago. This was during the Late **Jurassic period** of the **Mesozoic era**.

WHAT WAS THE BRACHIOSAURUS?

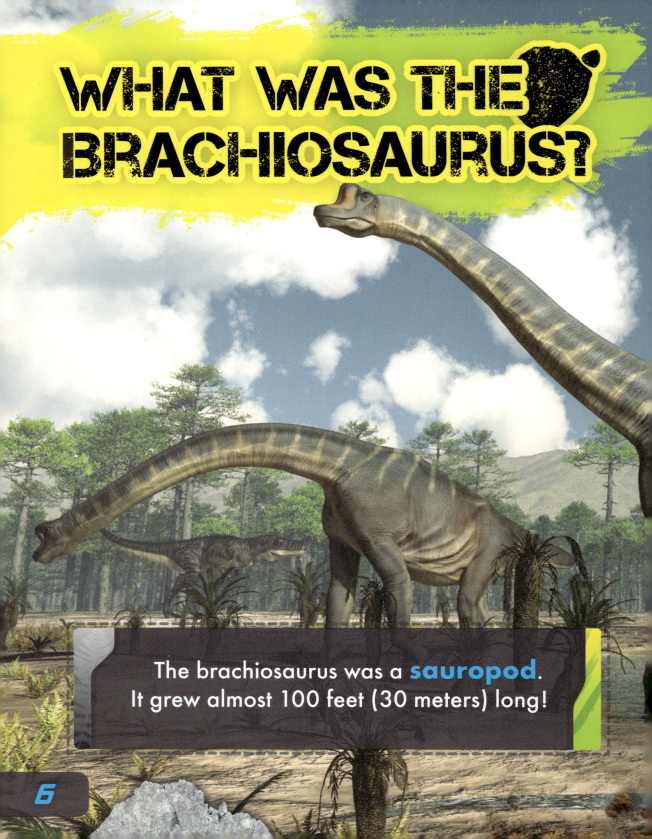

The brachiosaurus was a **sauropod**. It grew almost 100 feet (30 meters) long!

Its neck alone stretched 30 feet (9 meters) long. A long tail helped the dinosaur balance.

GIANT HEART

The brachiosaurus needed a large heart to pump blood up its long neck. Its heart likely weighed over 800 pounds (363 kilograms)!

SIZE CHART

25 feet (7.6 meters)
15 feet (4.6 meters)
5 feet (1.5 meters)

The brachiosaurus was built like a giraffe! It had long front legs and short back legs.

⚠️ NAME GAME

Brachiosaurus is a Greek word that means "arm lizard."

Its longer front legs helped the dinosaur hold its head up. This let it reach food other animals could not reach.

The brachiosaurus had a **bulge** on top of its head. The bulge held a large airway.

It helped the dinosaur breathe easily while it ate from trees.

DIET AND DEFENSES

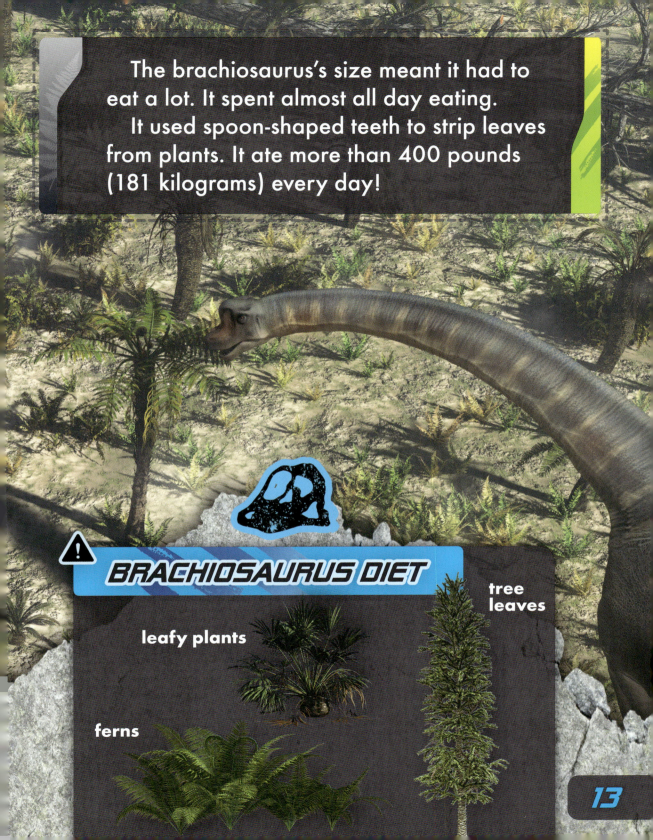

The brachiosaurus's size meant it had to eat a lot. It spent almost all day eating. It used spoon-shaped teeth to strip leaves from plants. It ate more than 400 pounds (181 kilograms) every day!

BRACHIOSAURUS DIET

tree leaves

leafy plants

ferns

An adult brachiosaurus did not have many **predators**. But its young could be **prey** to enemies.

herd

The dinosaur likely lived in **herds** to keep young safe.

FOSSILS AND EXTINCTION

Earth began to change during the Late Jurassic period. The brachiosaurus could not survive. It went **extinct**.

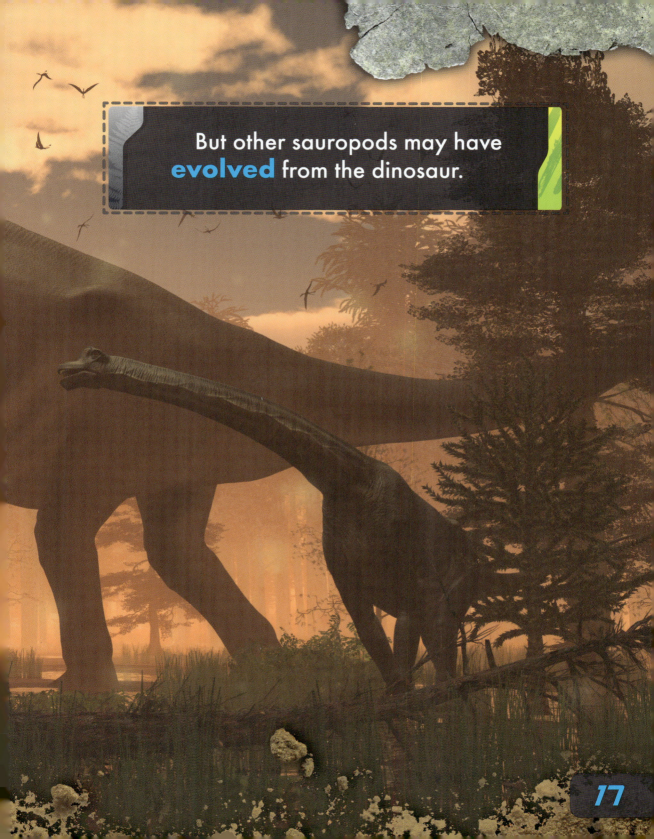

But other sauropods may have **evolved** from the dinosaur.

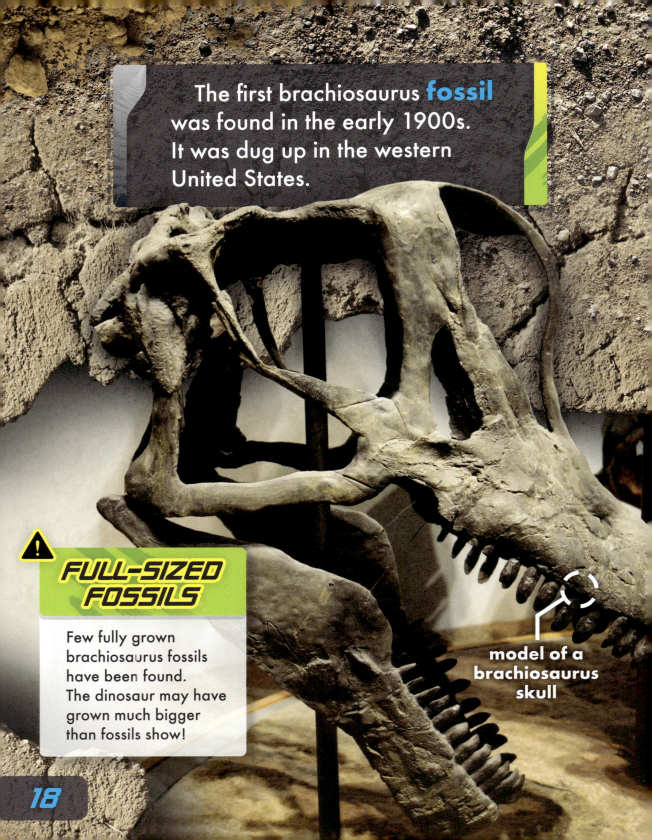

The first brachiosaurus **fossil** was found in the early 1900s. It was dug up in the western United States.

⚠️ **FULL-SIZED FOSSILS**

Few fully grown brachiosaurus fossils have been found. The dinosaur may have grown much bigger than fossils show!

model of a brachiosaurus skull

BRACHIOSAURUS FOSSIL MAP

North America

Europe

Africa

South America

KEY
fossil site

More fossils have been found since. Scientists study them to learn about the life of this huge dinosaur!

GET TO KNOW THE BRACHIOSAURUS

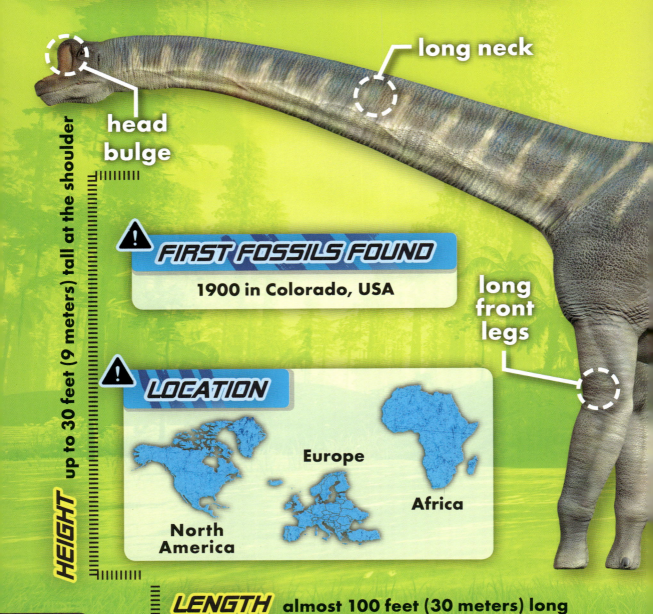

- head bulge
- long neck
- long front legs

HEIGHT up to 30 feet (9 meters) tall at the shoulder

FIRST FOSSILS FOUND
1900 in Colorado, USA

LOCATION
North America, Europe, Africa

LENGTH almost 100 feet (30 meters) long

ERA
157 million to 152 million years ago during the Late Jurassic period

Mesozoic era
- Triassic
- Jurassic
- Cretaceous

WEIGHT
up to 75,000 pounds (34,019 kilograms) = 6 elephants

FOOD
- leafy plants
- tree leaves

21

GLOSSARY

bulge—a rounded lump that sticks out

evolved—changed slowly, often into a better, more complex state

extinct—no longer living

fossil—the remains of a living thing that lived long ago

herds—groups of dinosaurs that lived and traveled together

Jurassic period—the second period of the Mesozoic era that occurred between 200 million and 145 million years ago; the Late Jurassic period began around 163 million years ago.

Mesozoic era—a time in history in which dinosaurs lived on Earth; the first birds, mammals, and flowering plants appeared on Earth during the Mesozoic era.

predators—animals that hunt other animals for food

prey—animals hunted by other animals for food

sauropod—a four-legged dinosaur that ate plants and lived during the Jurassic and Cretaceous periods; sauropods had small heads and long necks and tails.

TO LEARN MORE

AT THE LIBRARY

Doeden, Matt. *Could You Survive the Jurassic Period?: An Interactive Prehistoric Adventure*. North Mankato, Minn.: Capstone Press, 2020.

Hibbert, Clare. *Giant Dinosaurs: Sauropods*. New York, N.Y.: Enslow Publishing, 2019.

Sabelko, Rebecca. *Diplodocus*. Minneapolis, Minn.: Bellwether Media, 2020.

ON THE WEB

FACTSURFER

Factsurfer.com gives you a safe, fun way to find more information.

1. Go to www.factsurfer.com.

2. Enter "brachiosaurus" into the search box and click 🔍.

3. Select your book cover to see a list of related content.

INDEX

breathe, 11
bulge, 10, 11
evolved, 17
extinct, 16
food, 9, 11, 13
fossil, 18, 19
get to know, 20–21
head, 4, 9, 11
heart, 7
herds, 15
Late Jurassic period, 5, 16
legs, 8, 9
maps, 5, 19
Mesozoic era, 5

name, 9
neck, 4, 7
predators, 14
prey, 14
pronunciation, 4
sauropod, 6, 17
scientists, 19
size, 4, 6, 7, 13, 18, 19
tail, 7
teeth, 13
United States, 18
young, 14, 15

The images in this book are reproduced through the courtesy of: James Kuether, front cover, pp. 1, 4-5, 6-7, 8-9, 10-11, 12-13, 14-15, 16-17, 20-21; Etemenanki3/ Wikipedia, pp. 18, 19.